OCT 0 2

Louis Jolliet

Tristan Boyer Binns

Heinemann Library
Chicago, Illinois

© 2002 Reed Educational & Professional Publishing
Published by Heinemann Library,
an imprint of Reed Educational & Professional Publishing,
Chicago, Illinois

Customer Service 888-454-2279

Visit our website at www.heinemannlibrary.com

Design by Wilkinson Design
Maps by Kimberly Saar
Printed and bound in the U.S.A. by Lake Book Manufacturing, Inc.

06 05 04 03 02
10 9 8 7 6 5 4 3 2 1

Library of Congress Cataloging-in-Publication Data
Binns, Tristan Boyer, 1968-
   Louis Jolliet / Tristan Boyer Binns.
      p. cm. — (Groundbreakers)
Includes bibliographical references and index.
Summary: Presents an account of Jolliet's life and explorations and examines their impact on history and the world.
   ISBN 1-58810-597-0
   1. Joliet, Louis, 1645-1700—Juvenile literature. 2. Canada—Discovery and exploration—Juvenile literature. 3. Mississippi River Valley—Discovery and exploration—Juvenile literature. 4. Canada—History—To 1763 (New France)—Juvenile literature. 5. Mississippi River Valley—History—To 1803—Juvenile literature. 6. Explorers—America—Biography—Juvenile literature. 7. Explorers—France—Biography—Juvenile literature. [1. Joliet, Louis, 1645-1700. 2. Explorers. 3. Mississippi River—Discovery and exploration.] I. Title. II. Series.

   F1030.3 .B56 2001
   977'.01'092—dc21
                                              2001004032

Acknowledgments
The author and publishers are grateful to the following for permission to reproduce copyright material: pp. 4, 5, 10, 20, 21, 23, 24, 26, 39, 40 North Wind Picture Archives; pp. 6, 8, 14, 16, 25, 30, 41 The Granger Collection, New York; pp. 7, 17, 22 Hulton/Archive by Getty Images; p. 9 ©2001 Board of Trustees, National Gallery of Art, Washington D.C.; p. 13 Hulton Getty/Liaison Agency; p. 15 The New York Public Library; p. 18 National Maritime Museum Picture Library; p. 19 Austrian Archives/Corbis; p. 27 Kimberly Saar/Michigan Historical Center, Michigan Department of State; p. 28 Paul A. Souders/Corbis; pp. 29, 37 Wolfgang Kaehler/Corbis; pp. 31.

Cover photograph courtesy of North Wind Picture Archives.

Some words are shown in bold, **like this.** You can find out what they mean by looking in the glossary.

Contents

Who Was Louis Jolliet?

At the age of 28, an explorer named Louis Jolliet set off to find the Mississippi River. The government of New France, in what is now Canada, had given him the task of following it to its end. He needed to discover what body of water it emptied into. Was it a route west to the Pacific Ocean and Asia? Did it flow south through the whole continent, meeting the Gulf of Mexico? With only six fellow explorers and two canoes, Jolliet traveled 2,500 miles (4,000 kilometers) down the Mississippi and back. He found out that it flowed into the Gulf of Mexico. He also explored the fertile Illinois River valley, which later became an important farming area.

Jolliet's partner on his journey was Father Jacques Marquette. Marquette made a life out of setting up **missions** and preaching about God and Christianity. His efforts **converted** a great number of Native Americans to Catholicism.

Later voyages

Jolliet's travels did not end there, however. In later years, he mapped the first overland route to the Hudson Bay from Québec. He helped the French government learn about the

No pictures of Jolliet were drawn during his lifetime. Many modern artists have given us their ideas of what he may have looked like. This drawing, which shows him as a simple outdoorsman, is probably one of the most accurate.

English position in the Hudson Bay before they went to war. He made several maps that later helped countless sailors find their way safely. He even took a long trip up the eastern Labrador coast, meeting and trading with Inuit and describing their way of life. He was the first person to map this difficult coastline.

NATIVE AMERICAN NAMES

The word "canada" means "village" in the Huron Native American language. Many of the place names people use today come from Native American languages. The names of Chicago, Québec, Toronto, Kansas, and Susquehanna all come from different Native American languages. Even languages from tribes living close together often used a range of sounds and word types. They were as different as Russian, English, and French are today. This is why many of the words don't sound at all similar, even though they are all from Native American roots.

Towards the end of his life, Jolliet taught other people how to draw maps. He brought joy to people's lives through the organ music he played every winter in the cathedral of Québec. He and his wife Claire-Françoise had seven children in their long and happy marriage. Jolliet lived a full and interesting life and left us a legacy of discovery.

This is how Jolliet signed his name on letters and official documents.

Jolliet's Beginnings

Marie d'Abancourt and Jehan Jollyet already had two children when their son Louis was born in 1645. Louis was **baptized** on September 21, 1645, in Québec. The family lived in Beaupré, near Québec.

When Louis was born, there were only 2,000 French people living in Canada, which was called New France. Québec was a fairly small town. Most of the houses were made from logs, and the streets were unpaved. Many of the men worked as fur traders and trappers. They often fought with the neighboring Iroquois tribes. People didn't put much effort into building up good businesses and local food supplies. Instead, the settlers depended on France for government and supplies. They followed French fashions for clothes and shoes, even when they were wrong for the climate in New France. However, the Jollyet family had friends in New France who believed that New France should keep growing in size and strength.

Getting an education

Louis's father Jehan was a wheel and wagon maker who died when Louis was six years old. The family had never had much money. Then Louis's mother, Marie, married Godefroid Guillot, a rich merchant. The family probably moved to Québec after

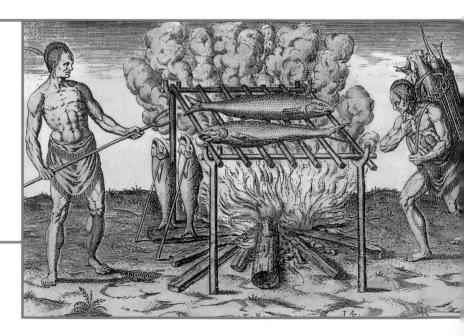

The Native Americans living in New France knew how to smoke fish. Before refrigerators were invented, food had to be smoked, salted, or dried to keep it safe to eat. The colonists preserved their food in the same way as the Native Americans did.

Québec was built on a rock that rises 300 feet (91 meters) above the St. Lawrence River.

their marriage. When Louis was ten years old, he went to a **Jesuit** college in Québec to study to become a priest. In those days, religion was very important to settlers in New France. They had to be Catholic and could only read religious books.

At college, Louis studied many subjects, including **cartography** and music. He loved to study and read books as well as play the organ. He worked his way through college as a musician. In 1665, his stepfather drowned, and Louis's mother married again. Once again, the family didn't have much money.

Life after college

Louis decided to leave the college in 1667. He told his teachers that he did not feel like he should become a priest after all. When he left the college, he had no money. He borrowed money from the bishop and went to France for about a year. No one knows why he went, but he did visit priests and people from New France. He may have spent time learning more about cartography from a master teacher.

When Louis got back to Québec, he decided to become a trapper and trader, like his older brother Adrien. Louis bought things like guns, cloth, tobacco, and bells to trade with Native Americans in 1668. But it seems that he didn't begin his life as a trapper until 1670.

SPELLING JOLLIET

No one knows why the spelling of Louis's last name changed. His father signed his name Jollyet, but Louis always spelled it Jolliet. Someone misspelled his name Joliet when copying a map he drew long ago. A city in Illinois is named after Louis, but it is spelled Joliet. Louis's brother Adrien changed the spelling to Joliette, and there is a town in Canada today that spells its name that way.

Trapping and Trading

Adrien Jolliet had always wanted to be a trapper and trader. He spent his childhood learning how to trap beaver and survive in the wilderness. Until Louis decided to become a priest, they had planned to work together. The Iroquois had captured Adrien when he was eighteen, and he learned their language before he was returned home two months later. He was one of the few Frenchmen who could speak Iroquois.

J. Grasset St. Sauveur made this engraving in the late 1600s. The Iroquois could be fierce fighters.

After an early successful career as a trapper and trader, Adrien was chosen in 1668 to go on an official **expedition** for New France. His assignment was to help look for copper on the southern border of Lake Superior, along the coasts of present-day Wisconsin and

RENÉ-ROBERT CAVALIER, SIEUR DE LA SALLE

Born in France in 1643, La Salle sailed to New France when he was only 23 and became a fur trader. La Salle became friendly with the Iroquois tribes near him and began exploring the area. He was looking for the **Northwest Passage.** La Salle was convinced that the Ohio River he had heard about from the Iroquois flowed into the Colorado River, and then into the Pacific. He became the first European to sail all the way down the Mississippi River in 1682. He claimed all the Mississippi River basin for France, naming the huge area of western North America "Louisiana." La Salle was killed by his own men in 1687 while trying to set up forts along the Mississippi River.

Michigan. He left in the spring of 1669. While he was away, Louis had to wait to start his **apprenticeship** as a trapper. He probably spent the time working in the family fur warehouses.

Meeting La Salle

In the autumn of 1669, Adrien met Sieur de La Salle, who was looking for the Ohio River. Adrien had with him an Iroquois prisoner who had helped him follow a Native American route back east from Lake Superior. Adrien told La Salle about the new route to the north and west.

La Salle chose to go a different way, and he may have found the Ohio River that winter. Adrien probably died on his way back to Québec, in 1670.

When his brother didn't return, Louis began to make trips west. He had a trader's permit, and he spent his time searching for Adrien and making maps of the places he saw. Often, he didn't bring back many furs. He developed a reputation as a good explorer, but not a good businessman.

George Catlin traveled all over the American frontier between 1831 and 1837, painting Native Americans and important moments in American history. This painting shows La Salle's expedition entering the Mississippi River on February 6, 1682.

Claiming Lands in the New World

When Christopher Columbus sailed from Spain in 1492, he was trying to find a direct route west to Asia, where Europeans traded with China and the Spice Islands. Trading for spices could make you rich, but it was very difficult. The ocean route east to Asia was dangerous, and many ships were lost each year. Some people thought that sailing west was impossible, because ships would just fall off the edge of the world. But others thought the world was round, so sailing west would eventually lead to Asia. Columbus had no idea that there was an entire continent blocking the way. At first, Europeans were disappointed that they couldn't get straight to Asia, but they quickly realized that this "New World" was rich in **natural resources.** They quickly began to explore it.

Looking for the Northwest Passage

Soon, explorers became convinced that there was a water route to Asia through North America. They called it the **Northwest Passage.** The English explorer John Cabot sailed to the northern areas in 1497 to look for it. He did not find it, but he found plenty of fish off Newfoundland, and he returned home after claiming the entire New World for England. The English weren't excited about the fish, and they were slow to

This map was drawn by Columbus's navigator, Juan de la Cosa, in 1500. All known lands are detailed, including the islands of the West Indies, which have Spanish flags on them. North America is the blue-green mass at the top left.

Jacques Cartier and Samuel de Champlain explored North America for France, paving the way for French **colonies** there.

settle the New World. But French fishermen in Brittany, the area of France right along the English Channel, heard about the cod in the New World. In the early 1500s entire fleets of French fishing ships sailed to Newfoundland.

Jacques Cartier was a French fisherman who came to Newfoundland for the cod. He discovered the Gulf of St. Lawrence in 1534 and claimed about half of the continent for France. He called this area New France because it reminded him of the landscape at home. He went on to explore the St. Lawrence River in 1535 and visited the places that would become the cities of Québec and Montréal. However, it would be years before French people would settle the land.

Colonies in the New World

North America is a huge continent. Hundreds of years ago, when the fastest ways to travel were sailing ships and horses, it seemed even bigger. European countries could only send small numbers of explorers and settlers to the New World. So even though each powerful country claimed large areas of land for themselves, they could only really defend smaller areas. Beginning in the early 1500s, Spain settled the southern areas of North America, including Mexico, Florida, and California. In the 1600s, England established colonies along the northeast coast, which grew into the 13 colonies that became the United States. France tried to settle along the East Coast, in places like North Carolina and Florida, but their colonies failed or were destroyed in battles. The real French holding in the New World was New France.

11

Champlain and New France

In 1603, nearly seventy years after Cartier claimed New France, Samuel de Champlain arrived there with French colonists. He promised to help the local Algonquin tribes along the St. Lawrence River in their struggles with their enemies, the Iroquois. In return, he received permission to settle the land and set up fur trading posts. Champlain sailed as far as the Lachine Rapids, near Montréal, and made friends with the Huron before turning back for France. He told the French king, Henry IV, about the opportunities for trapping beavers and farming the rich soil. He said that the French should be kind and helpful to their Native American neighbors.

Champlain strengthened his friendship with the Algonquin and Huron. He sent a Frenchman, Etienne Brulé, to live with the Huron. Brulé mapped the Great Lakes and other waterways as he traveled with the Native Americans. Champlain still hoped to find the **Northwest Passage** to Asia. But he had other duties as Governor of New France, and he couldn't leave Québec.

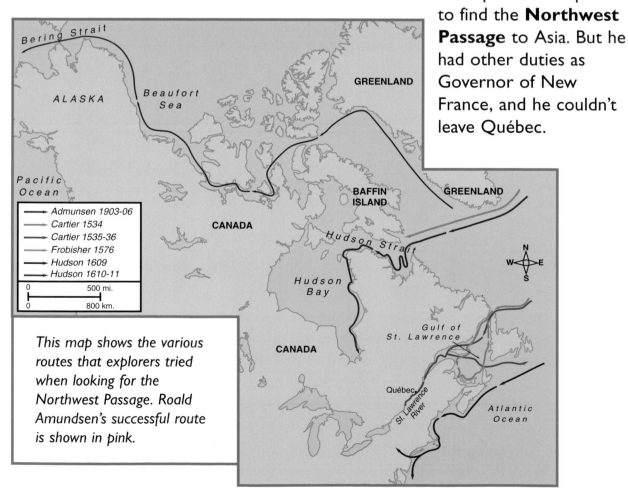

This map shows the various routes that explorers tried when looking for the Northwest Passage. Roald Amundsen's successful route is shown in pink.

Key:
- Admunsen 1903-06
- Cartier 1534
- Cartier 1535-36
- Frobisher 1576
- Hudson 1609
- Hudson 1610-11

0   500 mi.
0   800 km.

The battle in 1609 between the Huron and the Iroquois went quickly. The Iroquois had never seen guns before, so they lost even though they outnumbered the Huron.

Conflict with the English

The French settlements were successful, especially Québec. The beavers in the French lands north of the St. Lawrence River needed thicker coats to survive the colder weather, so they grew the best fur. The French fur trade was so profitable that the English, who held land to the south, became jealous. They made **treaties** with the Iroquois tribes, who attacked the Algonquin and Huron tribes on the north side of the river. The English then stole their furs. In 1609, Champlain helped his **allies,** the Algonquin and Huron, attack the Iroquois.

By 1629, France and England were at war. The English **blockaded** Québec in July, and Champlain was forced to surrender. He was taken to England as a prisoner but returned to Québec in 1633. The next year, he sent Jean Nicolet to follow Brulé's maps and find the Northwest Passage, but Nicolet was unsuccessful. When Champlain died in 1635, New France was over 1,500 miles (2,400 kilometers) wide, but the Northwest Passage was still just a dream.

THE NORTHWEST PASSAGE

Many explorers from different countries tried to find the Northwest Passage. This water route, connecting the Atlantic and Pacific Oceans, would make shipping much easier. No one knew where this route would begin or end, so different explorers tried different rivers and bays to see if they led across North America. The first was the English explorer John Cabot in 1497. Other explorers tried from both the Atlantic and Pacific sides to get through. The task was so difficult that it was not until 1906 that Norwegian Roald Amundsen became the first to sail all the way through the Northwest Passage.

The "Messipi"

Every French explorer knew about the river that most Native Americans in the area called "Messipi," which means "great river." It lay further west than Nicolet had traveled. Some people hoped that the Messipi turned to the west and flowed into the Pacific Ocean. If it did, then it was the **Northwest Passage.** But the Native Americans thought it flowed south. The French explorers also knew about the river that Spanish explorer Hernando de Soto discovered in 1541, which flowed into the Gulf of Mexico. It was also called the "great river" in Spanish— Rio Grande. However, no one knew that the two rivers were one and the same.

By 1665, France's settlements were being attacked and weakened by Iroquois. A French army went to war on the Iroquois and made peace with them after a few months. Now French **missionaries** could expand their territory once again. Explorers and trappers could travel in more safety from attack.

Hernando De Soto and his men were the first Europeans to see and cross the Mississippi River. They crossed it on June 18, 1541.

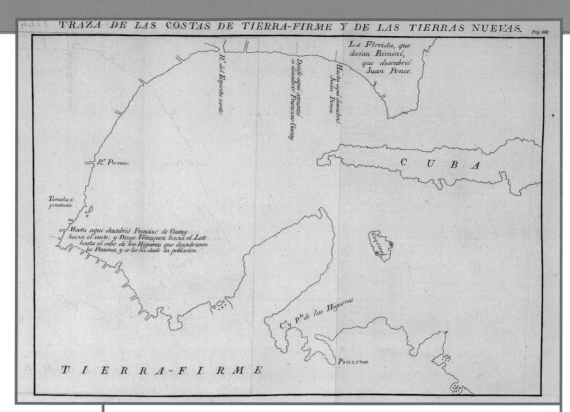

De Soto may not have been the first European to discover the Mississippi River. Alonzo Alvarez de Piñeda sailed and then sketched the Gulf of Mexico in 1520. His "Río del Espíritu santo" is the mouth of the Mississippi. But he may not have realized what he found.

Claiming lands for France

In 1671, Louis Jolliet was on a trapping trip in Sault Sainte Marie, where Lake Superior and Lake Huron meet in present-day Michigan. While there, he took part in an important ceremony on June 4. Simon Daumont de Saint-Lusson was acting for the French king, Louis XIV, and people were there from fourteen Native American nations. During the ceremony the French took possession of all lands from there to the Gulf of Mexico, and from the Hudson Bay to the Pacific Ocean. Jolliet was one of the people who signed the declaration.

But tensions were growing again between England and France. The government of New France was eager to see if the Messipi and the Rio Grande were the same river. If one river stretched from the north to the south of the continent, it would give the country that controlled it great power. That country could set up military posts along the river, creating a barrier to keep enemies from passing through. They could also control the flow of information up, down, and across the river, and influence the local Native Americans. La Salle had been sent to find the Mississippi in 1670, but he disappeared for three years instead.

Marquette and Jolliet

Jacques Marquette was born on June 1, 1637, into a well-known family in north-central France, in the town of Laon. When he was seventeen he began studying to become a **Jesuit** priest. He spent the next twelve years studying and teaching at Jesuit colleges. In 1666, he asked to be sent abroad. He went to Québec, then on to a **mission** on the St. Lawrence River, where he spent two years. He began learning Native American languages on this trip. Over the years, he learned about six **dialects** of at least two different languages.

Marquette's next stop, in 1668, was Sault Sainte Marie, where he talked with Native Americans as they fished and crossed between Lake Huron and Lake Superior. They told him stories about the "Messipi." The next year, he went to help at a new mission at Chequamegon Bay, near the western end of Lake Superior in present-day Michigan. He worked with the Huron and Ottawa tribes at the Mission of the Holy Ghost at La Pointe. While there, he met a member of the Illinois tribe and learned his language from him. Marquette decided that he wanted to travel down the "Messipi" and meet more of the Illinois tribe. His goal was to **convert** them to Christianity.

Father Marquette was not painted during his lifetime. However, many artists have guessed at what he looked like.

Meeting Jolliet

Marquette became a Jesuit priest on July 2, 1671, at an **ordination** service at Sault Sainte Marie. He was now called Father Marquette. (The French word for "Father" is "Père," so he is often known as "Père Marquette.") Jolliet was in the same area that summer, and they probably met. They may have even talked about a trip to explore the "Messipi." Father Marquette could not take such a trip alone, because he was a **missionary** and a **linguist,** not an explorer. Jolliet had the skills to guide and map an **expedition,** but he would need Father Marquette's language skills and experience with the Native Americans.

A Pipe of Peace.

Calumets were used by many of the Native American peoples of North America. They were used to show peaceful intentions to strangers who didn't speak the same language, and to seal agreements.

Jolliet went back to Québec, and Father Marquette went to start a new mission. The tribes living around his previous mission were at war with the Sioux, and he followed the Huron when they left the area. He set up Saint-Ignace Mission on Mackinac Island in the Straits of Mackinac, between Lake Michigan and Lake Huron in present-day Michigan. Soon, Saint-Ignace Mission moved to the northern shore of the Straits of Mackinac.

In Marquette's words:

"Would that I be ordered to set out for foreign lands. This has been the object of my thoughts since my earliest childhood... Previously, I felt inclined toward the mission in the Indies; today I would most gladly venture to whichever country it might please you to send me."

On August 4, 1667, he wrote about a skill that would be useful in the New World:

"I find no difficulty with languages unrelated to ours."

The Orders to Go

You can follow Jolliet's voyage on the maps on pp. 42-43.

In the summer of 1672, Louis Jolliet was officially told by the government to go look for the Mississippi River. He was told to find out where it emptied into the sea. No one is sure why he was chosen. He was known for his skills in **cartography** and surviving in the wilderness, but he had done nothing special so far in his life. However, the Governor said that he was someone who was "experienced in these kinds of discoveries and who had already been very near the river."

Although the government of New France officially sponsored the Mississippi **expedition,** it did not help pay for it. Some of its past expeditions had been expensive failures, so it was determined to lose no more money. Jolliet was told that he could make a profit on the journey by trapping and trading as he went.

Preparing for the voyage

Jolliet formed a partnership with seven other trappers, including his younger brother Zacharie. Jolliet agreed to pay for the expenses of the journey in return for more than half of the profits. The others would share the remaining profits.

In order to make good maps of their voyage, travelers had to keep computing their location. They used **compasses** *such as this one to find out what direction they were going.*

Three or four of his partners probably traveled with him, but no one ever wrote down who actually went on the expedition. Jolliet just said they went "with five other Frenchmen." Zacharie probably looked after the family warehouse while Louis was away.

Father Claude Dablon was in charge of all the **missions** in New France. He knew how much Marquette wanted to go down the Mississippi to meet and preach to the Native Americans there. So he gave Jolliet a letter for Marquette, saying that he was to go along with Jolliet on the journey.

Explorers used astrolabes to help navigate by using the positions of the stars. Along with compasses like the one on the facing page, they were the most advanced instruments of the day.

The departure

Jolliet set off with his men in October, 1672. His first stop, on December 8, was Saint-Ignace Mission. There, he told Marquette about their plans. They couldn't leave until the weather improved in the spring, so they had the winter to prepare. They packed corn and smoked meat to preserve it. They probably also brought items like beads, needles, and hatchets to trade or give to the Native Americans. In order to make good maps, they brought a compass and **astrolabe.** They also brought a map of areas that had already been explored, probably a map of Florida from 1656. They talked with Native Americans and made a preliminary map from what they learned of the area they were about to explore. By the middle of May, they were ready to start.

The Beginning of the Journey

You can follow Jolliet's voyage on the maps on pp. 42-43.

Jolliet and Marquette left Saint-Ignace in mid-May 1673, traveling in two canoes. They started on a route that had been used by the French before—across Lake Michigan, through Green Bay, and down the Fox River. At the beginning of June they left the Mascoutens Native American village, which was as far as Europeans had ever explored. From now on, they were traveling through uncharted territory.

The Mascoutens village helped by sending two guides with them as far as the end of the Fox River. There, they had to cross by land to the Wisconsin River. This kind of short land crossing is called a **portage.** Where they crossed is near the present-day city of Portage, Wisconsin.

In Dablon's words:

"...The road is broken by so many swamps and small lakes that it is easy to lose one's way ... we greatly needed our two guides, who safely conducted us to a portage of 2,700 paces, and helped us to transport our canoes to enter that river; after which they returned home, leaving us alone in this unknown country, in the hands of Providence."

Jolliet and Marquette paddled 118 miles (200 kilometers) down the Wisconsin River. They saw bison, which they had never seen before. They called them wild cattle. Near the end, they saw what looked like an iron mine. They reached the mouth of the Wisconsin River on June 15 and paddled into the Mississippi River for the first time.

Many artists have drawn their own versions of Marquette and Jolliet's trip.

This painting more likely shows what the canoe Marquette traveled in looked like. It had a small sail and was made of birch bark.

Frightening stories

The Native Americans Marquette talked with before their journey were scared of the Mississippi. They couldn't believe that Marquette would risk the trip. They told stories of vicious warriors, dangerous water full of monsters that would eat both men and canoes, a demon that swallowed travelers, and temperatures so high they would kill them. Marquette thanked them for the warning, but he didn't believe in the stories of monsters or demons. When he and Jolliet reached the Mississippi, no dangers leapt out at them.

FATHER MARQETTE'S JOURNAL

For about 250 years, historians thought that Father Marquette kept a journal of his trip. This journal was edited and passed on to the **Jesuit archives** by Father Dablon in 1677-78. But now experts think that Father Dablon wrote the whole "journal" himself. He probably used good sources, such as conversations with Jolliet and some of the other men who went on the voyage, letters from Jolliet and Marquette, Marquette's notes of the journey, Marquette's journal of his second trip to meet the Illinois, and maps made by Jolliet and Marquette. So even though Marquette probably didn't write the journal himself, it is certain that most of the information in it is accurate. Its original title, in French, is translated as "Report of the travels and discoveries of Father Jacques Marquette."

The Mississippi

YOU CAN FOLLOW JOLLIET'S VOYAGE ON THE MAPS ON PP. 42-43.

As Jolliet and Marquette paddled down the Mississippi River, they saw no people. They did see herds of bison, wildcats, and strange, huge catfish. The landscape and animals were new and interesting, but it wasn't until late in June that they met anyone. On that day they saw footprints and a narrow path leading away from the river. Marquette and Jolliet went alone to explore and met a village of about 3,000 Illinois people, called the Peoria.

The Peoria greeted them warmly and had a feast in their honor. The chief gave them a three-foot long peace pipe, called a **calumet.** He also gave Jolliet a young boy to take with him.

In the words of a Peoria chief:

"How beautiful the sun is, O Frenchman, when thou comest to visit us! All our village awaits thee, and thou shalt enter our cabins in peace."

According to Dablon, this is what the chief said when meeting Marquette and Jolliet.

A large group of about 600 Peoria saw them off on their journey. Jolliet began to teach the Illinois boy to speak French. Jolliet never wrote down his name, but he seems to have taken him along with him everywhere he went.

This engraving shows a Native American village much like the ones that Jolliet and Marquette visited.

This shows what an artist thought Jolliet and Marquette meeting the Peoria looked like.

The journey continues

Further down the Mississippi, they saw huge paintings on the rocks along the banks. The two paintings were the size of small cows and were done in green, red, and black. Jolliet later drew a picture that looked like a thunderbird, but Marquette described them as bearded, horned serpents. As soon as they passed them, the noise of rapids grew loud.

Where the Missouri River met the Mississippi, near present-day St. Louis, whole trees roared through the churning muddy water. It took great skill to make it past this point, but both canoes survived. The Missouri flowed from the northwest. The explorers had heard from Native Americans that it was possible to travel along this river towards California. Marquette hoped to preach to the people along the Missouri someday, but for now they continued down the Mississippi.

The Farthest South

You can follow Jolliet's voyage on the maps on pp. 42-43.

Between the Missouri and Ohio Rivers, the travelers had to navigate through a violent whirlpool. They saw another iron mine, with red clay that stained a paddle. Then the mosquitoes struck. They used the canvas sails as canopies for protection from the sun and the insects.

After drifting farther down the river, they came to a village on the riverbank. The villagers poured out of their homes, leapt into canoes, and came to attack the travelers. But when they saw one of Jolliet's men waving a **calumet,** they suddenly became friendly. They laid down their weapons and invited the travelers ashore.

The Spanish first met Native Americans in 1513 when Juan Ponce de León discovered Florida. He was killed when he returned in 1521.

In Dablon's words:

"They never see snow in their country, and recognize the winter only through the rains, which there fall more frequently than in summer."

Father Marquette's Journal had this to say about the Quapaw village.

With the Native Americans

The village was probably Quapaw, written by Marquette on his map as Metchigamea, but experts can't agree exactly at which village they stopped. They may have gone to Quapaw village and then on to one a little further down the river, Akamsea. Wherever they were, they shared the calumet and made friends with the people there. The Native Americans told them about Europeans who lived nearby—Spanish settlers in Florida. They had trade goods from the Spanish, and some from California. The Native Americans further down were unfriendly, and they were **allies** of the Spanish. They also said that it was just a short trip down to the mouth of the Mississippi.

Jolliet and Marquette talked about what to do. They now knew that the Mississippi did indeed drain into the Gulf of Mexico, and that it was not a route west to the Pacific Ocean. They decided that it was too risky to continue south, because the Spanish might kill them. If that happened, no one in Québec would hear of their discoveries. They had found out what they were sent to find out, so they turned for home, on about July 25. They had traveled as far as Arkansas, about 1,700 miles (2,740 kilometers).

The **latitude** measurements and sightings of landmarks recorded by Jolliet and Marquette are used now to help experts agree on their course. But those measurements were often not exact, and there are no first-hand written records of the journey. Also, the Native Americans they met had no written languages, so the spellings of their village names vary a lot. Experts have to use a wide range of sources to get at the truth, including reports from later travelers who tell about early meetings of Native Americans and Europeans.

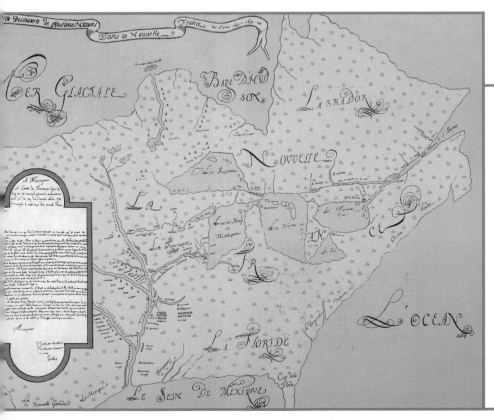

Jolliet drew the map this was based on from memory after he returned to Québec. Over time, the names he gave to places like Lake Frontenac changed to the Native American names, in this case, Lake Ontario. Frontenac was Governor of New France at the time, so Jolliet was honoring him by naming the lake after him.

Heading North

You can follow Jolliet's voyage on the maps on pp. 42-43.

Soon after they turned north, Native Americans with guns appeared along the banks of the river. The travelers displayed their **calumet,** and the Native Americans welcomed them and fed them. They were the Monsopelea tribe, living near present-day Memphis, Tennessee. Marquette gave them a letter, dated August 4, before he left.

From there, the explorers went north to the Illinois River. We don't know why they chose a different course back home, but they probably heard about this shorter, easier route from some of the Native Americans they had met.

Marquette's death

Father Marquette went back to preach to the Illinois tribes who had been so friendly during their trip. In October 1674 he left St. Francis Xavier **Mission** for the Kaskaskian village but was stopped by winter weather. He stayed near present-day Chicago all winter. When he arrived at the Kaskaskian village around Easter 1675 he was already sick. He preached to the Native Americans, then set out to return north to recover at his mission. However, he died of **dysentery** on the way, on May 18, 1675.

Father Marquette is buried near where he died, at Saint Ignace, not far from present-day Ludington, Michigan. A nearby river is named after him.

Although though they were paddling against the current, which is much harder, their trip home took no longer than the voyage out. About 200 miles (322 kilometers) along the way, they met the Kaskaskians. From the Illinois River they paddled along the Des Plaines River, and then they had a **portage** through present-day Chicago at the end of September. Jolliet wrote about the wealth of minerals they saw along the way. Finally, they traveled up Lake Michigan to Sturgeon Bay. They probably went together across a portage into Green Bay and reached the St. Francis Xavier Mission in mid-October.

Back in New France

Jolliet spent the winter and spring of 1673-74 at Sault Sainte Marie, taking care of business matters. Then he set off for Québec in May. He went down the Ottawa River and had almost reached Montréal when his canoe turned over. He lost all of his papers, including his journal and maps of the trip. The two men with him died, as did the young Peoria boy who traveled with him. He was rescued after swimming for four hours in the Lachine Rapids. He had left copies of his journal at the Sault Sainte Marie Mission, but they were lost in a fire.

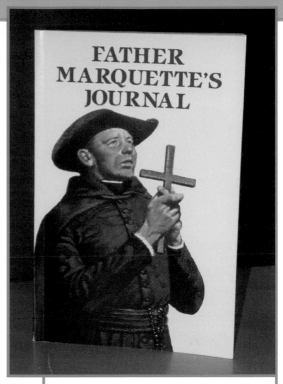

Father Marquette's journal was first published in 1681, and it can still be read today.

In Jolliet's words:

"I am much grieved over the loss of a ten year old ... He was of a good disposition, quickwitted, diligent, and obedient. He could express himself in French, and was beginning to read and write ... after four hours in the water, I was found by fishermen who never go to this place, and who would not have been there if the Blessed Virgin had not obtained for me this grace from God ... all I saved is my life."

Settling Down

Jolliet returned to Québec in 1674, but he was not greeted as a hero and brave explorer. Even though he had finished his assignment and made a full report to the government, he had lost his journal and map. He had also lost the furs he was bringing back to sell. He arrived broke, without hope for any income until Zacharie could send the furs that were stored in Sault Sainte Marie. But his report to the Governor inspired plans to settle the Mississippi Valley, which led to the French possession of Louisiana.

Adrien's widow had remarried twice. Her current husband thought that Jolliet owed her money because he had handled her property and business badly. Jolliet had even lost the canoe she had loaned him when it turned over in the rapids. Jolliet suddenly found himself **sued** and had to settle the case. Then

the widow and mother of one of his partners for the **expedition** sued him too. More lawsuits followed from other partners. Everyone was unhappy that the expedition had made so little money. The government settled all the cases by saying that the profits from the furs at Sault Sainte Marie would have to be divided equally.

Beaver fur was used to make hats. The fur was made into felt, which was shaped into a hat and then ironed to make it shiny. By 1731 more than 10,000 beaver hats were being made in America every year.

Starting a family

On a happier note, Jolliet had begun to **court** a woman before he left for the expedition. She was the daughter of the Bissots, who were close family friends. Claire-Françoise was eleven years younger than Jolliet was, but they were good friends. They grew closer during the winter and spring of 1674-75 and decided to get married. They signed a **marriage contract** on October 1, 1675. Many people witnessed the contract, including Claire-Françoise's mother, government officials, and businessmen. Jolliet's mother was also there, but she couldn't sign the contract because she had never learned to write. A week later Louis and Claire-Françoise were married in the Cathedral of Québec.

The Jolliet family moved into a small house in Québec. Jolliet built up his business, leaving Zacharie to handle the warehouse at Sault Sainte Marie. He even became the organist for the Cathedral of Québec. Claire-Françoise gave birth to their first son, Louis, on August 11, 1676. Jolliet finally seemed to have settled down.

The Cathedral of Québec, where Louis Jolliet married Claire-Françoise Bissot in 1675, has changed since the 1600s, but it is still standing.

More Exploring

Jolliet was not content to stay settled down for long. The year after his son was born, he applied to the French government for permission to settle the land along the Illinois River. He thought it looked like a wonderful place to begin a new settlement for New France. But he was not given permission. The colonial minister said, "The number of settlers in Canada should be increased before thinking of settlements elsewhere."

So the Jolliet family stayed in Québec. Louis bought a bigger house, and his wife's family moved in with them. He and Claire-Françoise had another son, Charles, on June 18, 1678. Jolliet acted as a teacher for Claire-Françoise's younger brothers and sisters. He worked hard in his businesses. With his father-in-law, he traded fish and seal oil along the coast. He shared a ship and the old fur trading business with his brother Zacharie. He also worked on revising the map of his trip down the Mississippi, which he was redrawing from memory. But he probably felt like he deserved more reward from the government than he was getting.

This engraving of the fishing industry in Newfoundland shows how Jolliet would have caught and preserved fish. Catching fish (C), drying fish (M), and pressing the oil from fish and seal (I) were all part of the business.

York Factory was the Hudson's Bay Company headquarters. It is now maintained by the Canadian government as a historic site, and many people visit it each year.

Rewarded by the government

Finally, in 1679, Jolliet and his father-in-law were given a series of islands along the northern bank of the St. Lawrence River by the government as a reward. Hunting and fishing on the islands brought in enough money for Jolliet to settle his debts, and for both of them to grow wealthy. But while they expanded business, tensions were growing again between the French and the English, especially over Hudson Bay. They thought it might lead to the Pacific, and they wanted the trading rights. Soon, France started to have problems getting furs in trade. The English were getting all the best furs from the Native Americans, while the French trading posts were quiet.

English ships could sail directly to the Hudson Bay from the Atlantic Ocean, but the French had no direct route north to the bay, either over land or by water. So the French government again asked Jolliet to help. One Frenchman had made the overland trip to the bay, but he was captured before he could get back. Jolliet was told to map a route and find out what the English were doing.

HUDSON'S BAY COMPANY

In 1670, King Charles II of England formed the Hudson's Bay Company. It controlled over 1.5 million square miles (2.4 million square kilometers), about one-third of present-day Canada. At first the company traded furs, but then it started exploring the surrounding area. Today, it is still one of Canada's largest companies. The first few decades of business were marked by battles with the French. For more than sixteen years, the French controlled four out of five of the Hudson's Bay trading posts. They had to give them back after a **treaty** in 1713 ended the war between France and England in Europe and North America.

To the Hudson Bay

YOU CAN FOLLOW JOLLIET'S VOYAGE ON THE MAPS ON PP. 42-43.

On May 13, 1679, Jolliet set out in canoes with eight men, including his brother Zacharie and his brother-in-law Guillaume. As Jolliet wrote, "After having traveled 343 **leagues** because of detours, although the distance is only 160 leagues in a straight line, and after 127 **portages,** some long and some short ... we came upon the bay all of a sudden." The first thing they saw was an English fort very close by. This was near present-day Fort Rupert, at the southern tip of James Bay. James Bay is the southern end of the Hudson Bay, so they had reached their goal. They didn't want to be attacked, so they fired a shot into the sky to warn the English of their arrival.

Three English soldiers hunting on the opposite bank greeted them, thinking they were Native Americans. When they realized they were French, they were still polite. Even when their countries were enemies, people living in the wilderness often had to be friendly to each other to survive. An Englishman and Jolliet started to talk together in Latin, since neither spoke the other's language. The French went to the English fort as guests and waited for the English governor, who was coming the next day.

Today the part of the Hudson Bay that Jolliet reached looks like this.

The Hudson's Bay Company had trading posts all over Canada. They offered a place for settlers and Native Americans to exchange goods and information.

Meeting the governor

Governor Bayley knew about Jolliet's **expedition** down the Mississippi and could speak French. He welcomed him by saying, "The English think highly of discoverers." Bayley didn't know that Jolliet was working as a spy on this mission, so he talked freely. Jolliet found out a lot about the fort's defenses, the trade with the Native Americans, and what the English planned to do to keep increasing their trade. Bayley said that the English paid up to four times more for furs than the French. They also went directly to the Native Americans, instead of making them travel to trading posts. He offered Jolliet a job, exploring and setting up a trading post. He wanted to pay Jolliet far more than the French ever did, but Jolliet was loyal to his country. He refused the offer.

When Jolliet and his men left, they were given some food for the journey home, with apologies that they could not be spared more. Jolliet returned to Québec on October 5, 1679, to find that his third son, Charles, had been born three weeks before. He had successfully mapped a route to the Hudson Bay and found out more than he expected about the English position.

In Jolliet's words:

*"There is no doubt that if the English remain in this bay, they will have control of all the commerce of Canada in ten years time .... When His Majesty decides on driving the English away from this bay and thus to become master of the whole country and of the beaver **pelt** trade, it will be an easy thing to point out by what means this is to be done and to show how the plan is to be carried out."*

33

Ups and Downs

The following spring, Jolliet was given the Île d'Anticosti (Anticosti Island) as a gift for "his discovery of the Illinois country ... and of the voyage which he has just made to Hudson Bay." Île d'Anticosti is at the mouth of the Gulf of St. Lawrence and vulnerable to any attackers heading for Québec. But it is huge—half the size of New Jersey—and surrounded by rich fishing. Jolliet built a house so that his family could spend summers on the island. They were the only people who lived there. He also had the rights to other islands nearby, called the Mingan **Archipelago.**

Now that Jolliet was finally getting the rewards he deserved, he made enemies. The **coureurs de bois** were a big problem. These trappers and traders worked illegally, without permits. They were accused of taking trade away from the government and legal trading posts. There were about 800 of them by this time, despite official efforts to get rid of them. One of Jolliet's former friends, Josias Boisseau, accused him of being a coureur de bois. He said that Jolliet was trading illegally in land owned by the king. For a year and a half Boisseau caused problems for Jolliet, until Boisseau was sent back to France and Jolliet was found to be innocent.

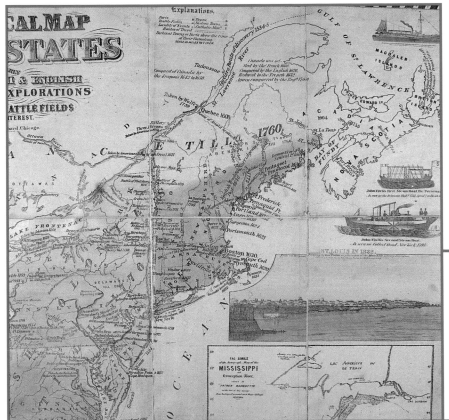

Mapmakers continued to use Jolliet's maps as a reference for years after his death. This map of New England includes a small copy of a map "drawn by Father Marquette."

Success at last

Jolliet's family grew and his business did well. He and Claire-Françoise had four more children between 1681 and 1685. Their house on Île d'Anticosti was not just a vacation home—it had storehouses for all the cod they dried and seal oil they made during the

The Île d'Anticosti still looks much like it did when Jolliet lived there.

summer. Jolliet even went on long fishing trips up the Labrador coast during the summer, leaving his family on Île d'Anticosti. The Jolliets spent winters in Québec, going to school and working in the business. Maps of the Mississippi and St. Lawrence Rivers that Jolliet drew or inspired were published in France.

Problems with the English

New France wasn't doing as well. Many of the settlers were very poor, without enough clothes and food for their families. There was even more tension with the English, leading to battles. The governor of Port Royal had surrendered to a British fleet led by Sir William Phips. Phips sailed to conquer Québec and Montréal next. His ships stopped at Île d'Anticosti in October 1690, while Jolliet and the older boys were away on a fishing trip. The English sailors captured Jolliet's wife, mother-in-law, young children, and servants. They also burned the buildings, destroyed the food, and stole anything of value. However, Phips failed to capture Québec. He traded his prisoners for English prisoners then fled back out to sea.

Jolliet tried to rebuild, but in 1691 English ships wrecked all of his holdings again. His wealth was gone, but he still wanted to explore. In the fall of 1693, he asked for permission to explore the Labrador coast and make a map of it. He set off in April 28, 1694, financed by a local merchant. He hoped to catch fish and get paid for his map, in order to pay for the trip.

The Labrador Expedition

YOU CAN FOLLOW JOLLIET'S VOYAGE ON THE MAPS ON PP. 42-43.

Jolliet's new **expedition** traveled by ship, not canoe. Seventeen men sailed with him, armed with twenty cannons. They traded at one of Jolliet's islands and spent a month helping to rebuild some of the burned buildings. Then Jolliet said good-bye to his family, except for his three oldest sons, who traveled with him. On June 9, 1694, they headed for Labrador.

The Inuit Jolliet met lived in houses similar to this one, made from caribou skins stretched on wood frames.

They made slow progress. Stopping to take the readings needed for mapping, and to trade for profit, slowed them down. After a month, they met some friendly Native Americans and saw houses that Inuit had lived in for the winter. They took a group of Native Americans north a short way, then traded with them before heading out again.

Friendly encounters

On July 12, Jolliet's men heard loud shots, like cannon fire. However, the noise wasn't attackers, but icebergs breaking up. They had been seeing icebergs for a few days and had to keep careful watch to avoid running into them.

36

Icebergs are especially dangerous for sailors because they are much larger than they appear. About 85% of their size is hidden underwater.

That same day, they saw an Inuit house big enough for twenty people to live in, but no one was there. Three days later they met two Inuit men in **kayaks.** Although they did not speak the same language, they agreed to trade. A week later the expedition met an entire Inuit village and spent five days trading and getting to know them. Jolliet wrote about how they lived, what they looked like, what they wore, and what they ate. The French and the Inuit sang and danced for each other. The Inuit were a little shy and careful. They didn't want to go on Jolliet's ship, but they were very friendly.

Turning back

As Jolliet's men continued north, they met more Inuit. They also saw Spanish goods, which meant that the Inuit had traded with them, too. The expedition continued to map the small coves and bodies of water along the coast, while meeting and trading with many Inuit. By the middle of August they were ready to head home. The trading was not rich enough to pay for the sailing costs, and their anchor cables were weak. Jolliet worried about icebergs and bad weather. But the trip home was slow, since they stopped to catch fish. By October, the Jolliet family was reunited in Québec.

In Jolliet's words:

*"I wrote down several words of their language which seems rather easy to learn. They were always cheerful, **affable,** and inclined to laugh; and they invited us back to their huts several times."*

*"I saw in their cabins three large cauldrons in which they were cooking meat. They have few cauldrons .... Their beds are one foot above the ground; the blankets are **pelts** of caribou, seals, bears and of other animals. Their cabins are neat and clean. In the summer they are circular in form and covered with seal hide, really tents .... They also make earthenware pots large and small, in which they refine oil and cook food."*

Jolliet's Final Years

In 1693, the ship *Corossol* hit a rock near one of Jolliet's islands in the Mingan **Archipelago.** It sank so fast that very few people survived. Jolliet had sent a map of the area to the French government back in 1685, but pilots had never used it. A newer map that wasn't as good led to the *Corossol's* wreck. In 1694, the government of New France tried to get permission from the king of France to map the St. Lawrence Gulf and River again, because sailors and pilots were scared after the big wreck. Finally, in 1695, the king ordered the government to hire Jolliet and pay him well to make the map. He was also paid for the map he had sent in 1685.

This statue of Jolliet shows him on horseback, wearing expensive clothes. However, he spent most of his time traveling by canoe or ship.

Return to France

In November 1695 Jolliet was asked to pilot a ship that was late in sailing back to France. The St. Lawrence River was very dangerous at that time of year, so no one else wanted to do it. Jolliet had sailed that stretch so many times, on trips to Île d'Anticosti and his other islands, that he was the perfect man for the job. He easily made the voyage and spent the winter in France.

Jolliet went to Paris and asked to be made professor of hydrography, which is the science of measuring and describing seas, lakes, and rivers. His request was granted a year after he returned—on April 30, 1697, Jolliet was made Royal Hydrographer at Québec.

This statue seems more like Jolliet. He has a walking stick and is looking out as if seeing something new.

On the same day he was given another property, now called Joliette, south of Québec. He spent the winters teaching and making maps in Québec. One of them, showing pilots the safe way past Île d'Anticosti and through the Gulf of St. Lawrence, was dated 1698.

Jolliet's death

The last date when Jolliet was known to be in Québec was May 4, 1700. Soon after that, he probably left for his summer home on Anticosti. He most likely planned to spend the summer as usual—fishing, trading, and making notes for new maps. But sometime before September 15 he died. Historians do not know how or where he died. No one has found his grave. But there was a special mass said for him in the Cathedral of Québec on September 15, in thanks for his having played the organ there for so many years.

After Jolliet's debts were paid, his widow was left poor. When Claire-Françoise died, she was penniless. His six surviving children and his grandchildren eventually continued to receive profits from his holdings and inherited some of the land themselves.

Jolliet's Legacy

*La Salle fulfilled Jolliet's dream of traveling to the mouth of the Mississippi, but his plans for French **colonies** along the river ended in failure.*

Jolliet was the first important explorer of European descent to be born in North America. His achievements have been recognized and written about ever since he first traveled the Mississippi River. In 1681, Father Dablon's account of the journey, Father Marquette's Journal, was published in Europe. During the seventeenth and eighteenth centuries, Jolliet was more famous in Europe than any other Canadian.

After Jolliet and Marquette paddled down the Mississippi, it was opened up for other Europeans to explore and settle. In 1682, La Salle traveled all the way down the Mississippi River. He named the huge area along the river and to the west "Louisiana," in honor of the French king, Louis XIV. In 1803, President Jefferson bought Louisiana from the French. This was called the Louisiana Purchase. The addition of this land meant that the United States of America now stretched from the Atlantic Ocean to the Pacific Ocean. The western lands were opened up to settlement, and the Oregon Trail soon brought thousands of settlers to new lives in California and Oregon.

CHICAGO

On their return trip, Jolliet and Marquette were the first Europeans to travel through the area that is now the city of Chicago. Later, two Native American villages grew up there. Father Francois Pinet, a **Jesuit missionary,** founded a **mission** in 1696, but it only lasted until 1700. Chicago wasn't permanently settled until 1779, when Jean Baptiste Point du Sable, an African American pioneer, and his Native American wife built a home near the present-day Michigan Avenue bridge.

Changing the Mississippi Valley

Jolliet had wanted to settle the Illinois country, but he wasn't allowed to. La Salle began the first European settlement there. But today the city of Joliet, Illinois, is named after Jolliet, who camped near there on his way back up the Mississippi in 1673.

The Native Americans living along the Mississippi were changed forever by the coming of the Europeans. Some were able to adapt their way of life as new technology and trade goods became common. However, many more were forced off their lands or killed by battles and European diseases.

Jolliet may have experienced ups and downs during his lifetime, but he certainly helped people who came after him. His travels to Hudson Bay and up the Labrador Coast had less historical value than his trip down the Mississippi, but his reports were valuable to the government at the time. Many sailors and merchants used his maps to guide them safely through difficult or unknown waters.

This is the map that was published in 1681 with Father Marquette's account of the **expedition.**

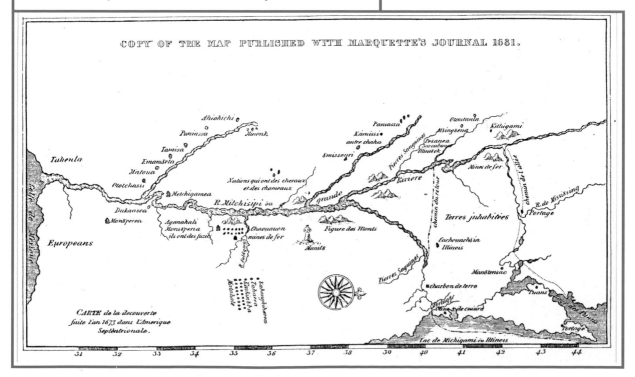

Maps

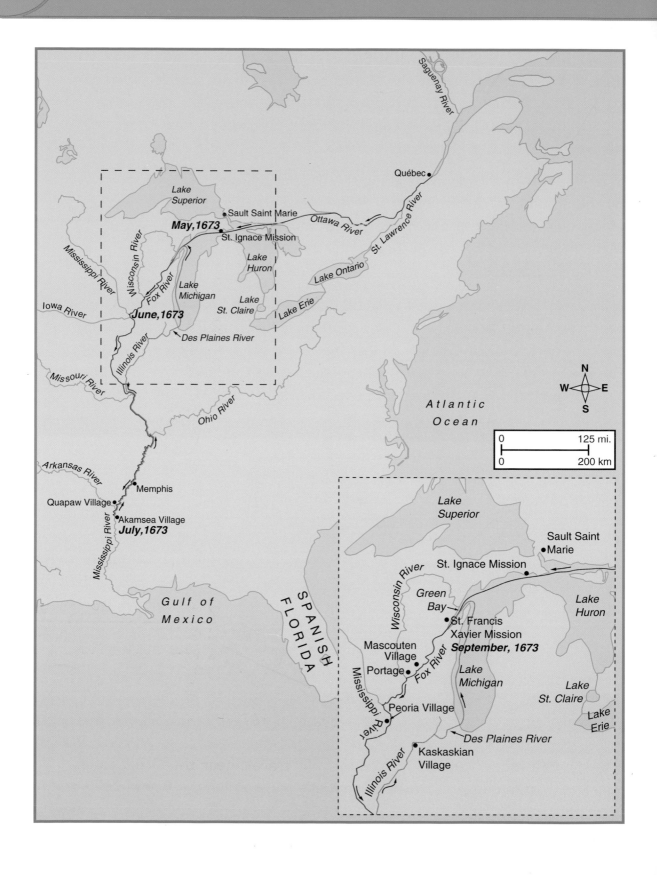

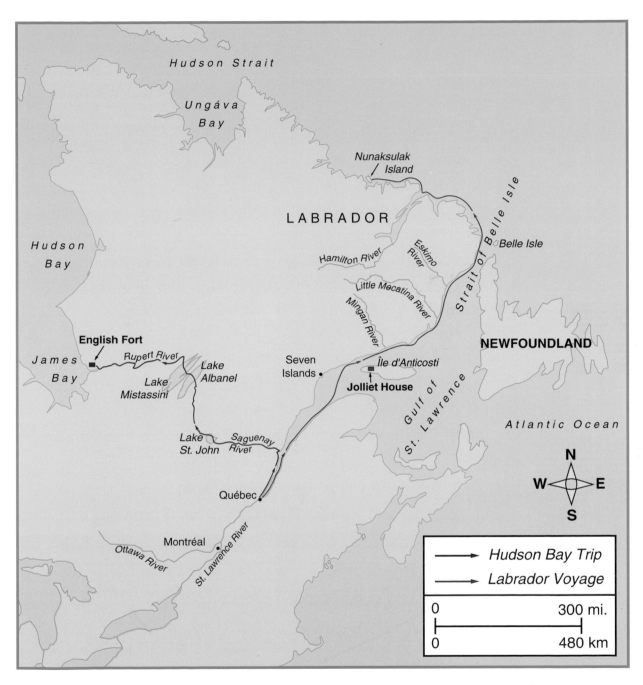

The map on the left shows Jolliet's voyage of 1672–73 with Father Marquette. Their trip out is shown in red, and their return is in orange. The smaller inset map gives a more detailed picture of their travels near the Great Lakes.

On the map above you can follow Jolliet's trip to Hudson Bay in 1679 and his travels along the Labrador Coast in 1694. You can also see the Île d'Anticosti, where Jolliet and his family lived for many years.

Timeline

1645	Louis Jolliet is born near Québec, probably in Beaupré, in late September. He is **baptized** in Québec on September 21.
1655	Jolliet begins attending a **Jesuit** college in Québec in order to become a priest.
1663	Jolliet receives minor orders in the Catholic Church.
1667	Jolliet leaves the Jesuit college after deciding not to become priest. He goes to France, probably to study **cartography.**
1668	Jolliet returns to New France and decides to become a trapper and fur trader.
1671	Jolliet attends the formal possession of lands ceremony at Sault Sainte Marie on June 4. He probably met Father Jacques Marquette here.
	By September, Jolliet is back in Québec, with approval from Governor Frontenac but no funding for a trip to explore Mississippi.
1672	On October 1, Jolliet signs a partnership agreement with six other trappers and traders.
	On December 8, Jolliet arrives at the Saint-Ignace **Mission** at Mackinac.
1673	Jolliet's **expedition** begins its journey (May).
	The expedition reaches the Mississippi River (June 15).
	Jolliet reaches the end of the journey and turns for home (July).
	Jolliet's party arrives at St. Francis Xavier Mission, having traveled 2,500 miles (4,000 kilometers). Father Marquette remains there (September).
1674	Jolliet returns to Québec. In August, his canoe overturns in the Lachine Rapids, so he loses his diary and the map of the journey.
1675	Jolliet marries Claire-Françoise Bissot.
1676	Jolliet requests permission to set up a trading station in Illinois country. When permission is refused, he forms a company trading fur on north shore of the St. Lawrence.
1679	Jolliet is granted the Mingan **Archipelago** in the lower St. Lawrence River. French officials order him to go to Hudson Bay to spy on the English.

	Jolliet leaves for Hudson Bay with seven companions (April 13).
	Jolliet returns to Québec (October 5).
1680	The Île d'Anticosti is given to Jolliet as a reward for his service to France. He builds a fort there and uses it as a summer home.
1681	A map drawn by Jean-Baptiste-Louis Franquelin of Jolliet and Marquette's discoveries is published in Paris.
1685	Jolliet sends his map of the St. Lawrence River and gulf to the Ministry of the **Colonies** in France.
1690	Ile d'Anticosti is captured by the English. Jolliet's wife and children are taken prisoner but released shortly after.
1694	Merchant François Viennay-Pachot agrees to fund an expedition to the Labrador coast to explore, make maps, fish, and hunt.
	Jolliet and seventeen men leave for the Labrador coast (April 28).
	Jolliet returns to Québec with detailed notes and sketches about the Labrador coast (October).
1695	Jolliet is hired to make a new map of the St. Lawrence River and gulf.
1697	Jolliet is appointed Professor of Hydrography at the College of Québec. He is given property south of Québec that is now called Joliette (April 30).
1700	Louis Jolliet dies some time between May and October.

More Books to Read

Harmon, Daniel E. *Jolliet & Marquette: Explorers of the Mississippi River.* Broomall, Penn.: Chelsea House Publishers, 2001.

Isaacs, Sally Senzell. *America in the Time of Pocahontas.* Chicago: Heinemann Library, 1999.

Santella, Andrew. *Sieur de La Salle.* Chicago: Heinemann Library, 2002.

Glossary

affable friendly and easy-going

ally person or country that unites with another for a common purpose

apprenticeship period of time when a person learns by practical experience how to do a job

archipelago group of islands

archive place where public records or historical papers are saved

astrolabe small instrument that is used to calculate the position of objects in the sky in relation to each other

baptize to sprinkle someone with water as part of a ceremony of receiving into the Christian church

blockade to close off a place to prevent people or supplies from going in or out

calumet pipe that serves as a symbol of peace and a safeguard against harm

cartography science of drawing maps

colony group of people sent out to settle a new territory

convert to persuade someone to change their religious beliefs, either by choice or by force

coureur de bois trapper who traded illegally, defying the government's orders that all trappers must have permits

court to pay attention to someone with the intention of marrying them

dialect local variation of a language

dysentery serious disease that causes severe diarrhea

expedition trip taken to discover new places

Jesuit Catholic order founded by Ignatius Loyola in 1534. Jesuits traveled around the world founding missions, trying to convert people to Catholicism.

kayak single-person canoe

league measure of distance, between 2.4 and 4.6 miles (3.9 to 7.4 kilometers) long, that was used in the past

latitude distance north or south of the equator

linguist person who speaks and understands a number of languages

marriage contract legal document that serves as an agreement to marry

mission place built and run by priests to convert people to its religion

missionary someone sent to convert people to his or her religion

natural resource something found in nature that is valuable to humans

Northwest Passage water route across the continent of North America

ordination religious ceremony that makes a person a priest

pelt skin and fur of an animal

portage short route by land either between two bodies of water, or past rapids or other stretches of water too dangerous to sail through

sue to take someone to court in order to get money owed by them or to settle a disagreement

treaty agreement between two or more countries or nations

Index